LIVING *through* HISTORY

Native Americans

The Indigenous Peoples of North America

Fiona Reynoldsc

Heinemann

Heinemann Educational Publishers
Halley Court, Jordan Hill, Oxford, OX2 8EJ
a division of Reed Educational & Professional Publishing Ltd
Heinemann is a registered trademark of Reed Educational & Professional
Publishing Ltd

OXFORD MELBOURNE AUCKLAND
JOHANNESBURG BLANTYRE GABORONE
IBADAN PORTSMOUTH NH (USA) CHICAGO

© Heinemann Educational Publishers 2000

First published 2000

ISBN 0 435 31015 1
02 01
10 9 8 7 6 5 4 3 2

Designed and typeset by Paul Davies and Associates
Illustrated by Pip Shuckburgh and Phil Burrows

Cover design by Wooden Ark Studio, Leeds

Printed and bound in Spain by Edelvives

Photographic acknowledgements
The authors and publisher would like to thank the following for permission to
reproduce photographs: Amon Carter Museum: 4.5A; Beinecke Library, Yale
University: 3.6A; Brian and Cherry Alexander: 2.3B; Bruce Coleman: 2.1A, 2.5A;
Corbis: 1.1A; David Neel: 3.7A; Erich Lessing/Art Resource New York/Museum
of Mankind, London: 3.8B; Idaho Historical Society: 4.3C; JR Cox/National
Archives of Canada: 2.8B; National Geographic Image Collection: 1.2B, 3.2C;
Nelson-Atkins Museum of Art: 4.8A; Popperfoto: 5.1A; Royal Ontario Museum:
3.3A, 4.1A; Sid Richardson Collection: 4.2A; Smithsonian Institution: 1.2C, 1.3A,
3.6B, 3.7B, 3.8A, 4.4B, 4.7A, 4.9A

Cover photograph: Corbis/Michael T. Sedani

Written acknowledgements
In some sources the wording or sentence structure has been simplified to
ensure that the source is accessible.

E. Cones, The History of the Lewis and Clark Expedition, New York, 1893: 3.2A,
4.1B, 4.3A, 4.3B, 4.4A, 4.7B; P. Freuchen and F. Salomonsen, The Arctic Year,
Jonathon Cape, 1958: 2.5B, 2.6C; J. Hook, American Indian Warrior Chiefs,
Firebird Books, 1989: 4.8B; A.M. Josephy Jr., 500 Nations, Alfred A. Knopf, New
York, 1994: 1.2A, 4.9B; J. Meares, Voyage to the North West Coast of America,
London, 1970: 3.3B; V. Stefansson, My Life With Eskimos, Harrap, 1924: 2.3A,
2.4B, 2.8A; D. Tenness, The Indians of Canda (Government Report), National
Musem of Canada, 1932: 2.2C

CONTENTS

Native Americans

1.1 WHERE DID THE NATIVE AMERICANS COME FROM?

For hundreds of thousands of years human beings have inhabited Africa, Europe and Asia. These people were originally hunter-gatherers. They followed herds of animals for mile after mile across vast open lands.

At some time, probably about 20,000 to 40,000 years ago, human beings from the north-east corner of Asia, now called Siberia, carried on following herds of mammoth and bison across a piece of land called Berengia into what is now North America.

Berengia used to link Asia to North America. This was because, at different times throughout history, world temperatures

There were only certain times when the land bridge of Berengia was open and the way south into America was not blocked by ice. Whenever these times were, it is certain that by about 11,000 years ago both North and South America were settled because remains of human settlements have been found in the southern tip of South America.

Archaeologists and language experts have tried to trace the movements of these early settlers in America. Archaeologists have studied stone tools and weapons, animal bones and human bones at different sites. Some stone choppers and scrapers date back about 20,000 to 30,000 years.

▨	ice sheets
•	remains of human settlement 11,500 years ago
→	route of human beings into America

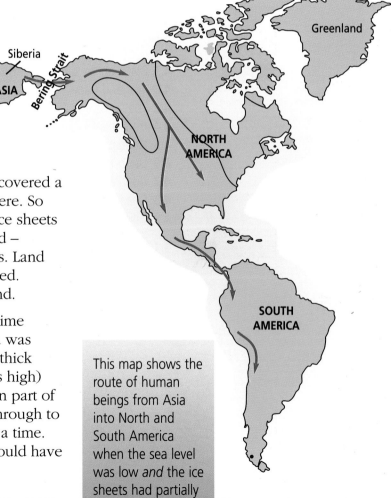

This map shows the route of human beings from Asia into North and South America when the sea level was low *and* the ice sheets had partially melted.

have changed and ice sheets have covered a great deal of the northern hemisphere. So much water was locked up in the ice sheets that sea levels fell all over the world – sometimes by as much as 85 metres. Land that is now under water was exposed. Berengia was one such piece of land.

However, there was a snag. Some time during the Ice Ages when Berengia was exposed, the sheets of ice were so thick (possibly as much as 1.6 kilometres high) that they covered all of the northern part of America. Then there was no way through to the south for thousands of years at a time. Any people hunting in Berengia would have had to turn back into Asia.

Source A

The Bering Strait, shown in this photograph, is a stretch of water that separates Asia from North America where the land bridge of Berengia used to be. It was named after Vitus Bering, a Danish navigator who explored the coast of Alaska.

The languages of Native Americans

By the time the Europeans first came to America in the early sixteenth century, there were probably some 200 Native American languages being spoken. Each one was different and one tribe could not understand the language of the neighbouring tribe next door. However, many of the languages were related in the same way that German, Icelandic and English are related. This means that these tribes came originally from the same people.

The Aleut-Inuit languages are very different from other sets of languages in North America. They are spoken by people who settled in the far north of North America and on the edge of Greenland. This is one of the ways we can tell that these people came to America long after the others. Although not all experts studying the languages of the area agree, some of them think that there were three main times (or waves) when people crossed from Asia to America either by walking overland or by sea.

The three main times when people crossed from Asia to America

- First wave (before 11,500 years ago).
- Second wave (about 9000 years ago).
- Third wave – Aleut and Inuit (about 4000 years ago).

Things to do

1 Why did sea levels fall when there were huge ice sheets?

2 What was Berengia?

3 How do we know about the people who settled in America?

4 How do we know that the Aleut and Inuit came at a different time from the first two waves of people?

5 By the time the third wave arrived, the ice sheets were melting fast. How might these people have travelled to America?

6 Why do you think no one can say for sure how they travelled?

When Christopher Columbus landed on an island in the West Indies in 1492, he thought he had landed in India, so he called the inhabitants 'Indians'. In fact he was the first European to set foot in what later became known as the Americas. This is what we today call North America, South America and the islands around those two continents. Other explorers also called the native peoples of the Americas 'Indians', although they in fact lived nowhere near India. Despite what we sometimes say neither Columbus, nor any other European, could actually claim to have 'discovered' America. You cannot discover a continent that is already inhabited. For example, if you were to sail from America to Britain today, you would not be *discovering* Britain because it is already inhabited by people. In this book you will be studying the native peoples of North America, or 'America' as many people call it.

Populations in North and South America

Estimates vary, but many experts think that somewhere between 20 million and 50 million people were living in the Americas by 1492. Some put the estimate even higher. The numbers were a considerable proportion of the entire world population of human beings at this time. For example, there were cities in Mexico – which is in the south of North America – that were far bigger than London and many other European cities.

Civilisations

It was around the area of present day Mexico that the Mayans and the Aztecs lived. The Aztecs built cities, temples and **irrigation works** so that they could farm and support a large population. Further north, in Ohio, the civilisation of the Hopewell people had flourished for hundreds of years before Columbus came to America.

All over the continent there were farmers, hunter-gatherers, fishermen, craftsmen and traders from Alaska to Florida and on to South America. In South America, the Inca people numbered around 12 million. They built 17,000 kilometres of roads; they terraced hillsides for farming; they built canals to irrigate the land: and they used llamas (animals related to camels) to carry their loads over the mountains. They were great organisers and, like the Mayan, they knew a lot about mathematics and **astronomy**.

The wheel and the plough

All of these lands were not empty in 1492. So how was it that the Native Americans did not repel the European invaders? The answer is that their technology was inferior. There were two crucial inventions that did not exist in the Americas: one was the wheel, and the other was the plough.

Both these inventions are at the root of developments in agriculture and in transport that in Europe and Asia led to the growth of powerful civilisations. Early explorers of the Americas said the lack of the wheel and the plough there showed a primitive, less intelligent race. However, there is no point in inventing the wheel (apart from the limited use of a wheelbarrow) unless you have animals, such as horses and oxen, to pull carts – and the same thing goes for the plough. There were no native animals on the American continent capable of pulling ploughs and carts, so the native people had to develop in a different way.

Source A

An extract from a book in which Tall Oak of the Narragansett Tribe describes the names given to the first Europeans to arrive.

When the first Europeans arrived, Columbus and his crew, he came and called us Indians, because of the obvious reason, he thought he was lost in India. But what did we call ourselves before Columbus came? That's the question so often asked. And the thing is in every single tribe, even today, when you translate the word that we each had for ourselves, without knowledge of each other, it was always something that translated to basically the same thing. In our language it's Ninuog, or 'the people', the human beings. That's what we called ourselves. So when the pilgrims arrived here, we knew who we were, but we didn't know who they were. So we called them Awaunageesuck, or 'the strangers', because they were the ones who were alien, they were the ones that we didn't know, but we knew each other. And we were the human beings.

Things to do

1 Why did Europeans call the people of the Americas 'Indians'?

2 What evidence is there that a number of advanced civilisations existed in the Americas before 1492?

3 a What inventions were missing from the American continent?

   b What two possible explanations are given for this?

Source B

Ozette, a Makah village that was close to present-day Seattle on the west coast of North America. The Makahs were a tribe on the north-west coast of America.

Source C

The Inuit, who lived in very cold regions of North America, used sewing kits like this one to help them make protective garments.

We find out about people in the past by archaeological evidence and by written evidence. We have the things that Native Americans used to use (tools, bones, weapons, religious **regalia** and so on). But since most Native Americans did not use a written language we only know about them from what other people such as explorers, missionaries, traders, artists, politicians and so on have written. The difficulty with that is the writing comes from a different point of view. White people often wanted to make Indians seem either savage, primitive or untrustworthy to prove they had a good reason for taking their land away from them. But as the Indians were disappearing, other white people wanted to glorify them, in writing, in paintings and in praise of their art, their spiritual beliefs or their simple life.

Native peoples were quick to learn that white people laughed at their creation **myths**, religious observances and social customs. The white person's way was the only way (or so the white people thought). So the Native Americans often kept quiet, in case their ways of life were ridiculed or misinterpreted.

It is easier to look at what is left behind. After all, a tomahawk is a tomahawk and a totem pole is a totem pole. However, artefacts that are made of wood and other 'living' materials rot over a period of time, so not many survive from before the days of contact with white people.

The influence of 'the whites'

Once there was contact between Native Americans and white people, everything began to change. For instance, white people introduced metal. Metal tools meant better blades for everything from tomahawks to the tools for carving totem poles. And this is only one example. All people copy or learn from each other.

The Native Americans were influenced by the white people they came across and, from the sixteenth century onwards, adapted ideas in their art and everyday things. The Native Americans weren't only influenced by ideas. They were also influenced by things. The native peoples saw instantly how useful horses were to their way of life. Within a short period of time, they were using them for hunting and transport.

The horse could carry a bigger tipi than a dog, the range of hunting was expanded and the number of prey killed increased. So the arrival of white people raised the standard of living of the Native American.

The native people studied in this book

In this book we will look at three groups of native people.

First, we will learn about the Inuit in sections 2.1 to 2.8. The Inuit lived 'on the edge' in the coldest, most demanding terrain on earth. In these sections we will learn about their family life, the homes they lived in and how they hunted for food.

Next, we will learn about the native people of the north-west coast of America in sections 3.1 to 3.8. These people lived 'far from the edge' in an area of abundant food supplies and a mild climate.

Finally, we will look at the Nez Perce in sections 4.1 to 4.9. The Nez Perce lived 'between the edges' on the plateau between the north-west coast tribes and the plains tribes to the east. They fished, hunted and gathered, but they also went down to the Plains to hunt buffalo once they used horses. So they represent both a moderate life style and the change that swept the continent with the arrival of the whites with their horses and guns.

The Nez Perce were the only group of people we are looking at who used horses and lived in tipis.

Things to do

1 What are the two main ways of finding out about people in the past?

2 Why does that present a problem for historians studying Native Americans?

3 Why is it more difficult to find out what life was like as a Native American 200 years ago than it would be to find out about a British person's life at that time?

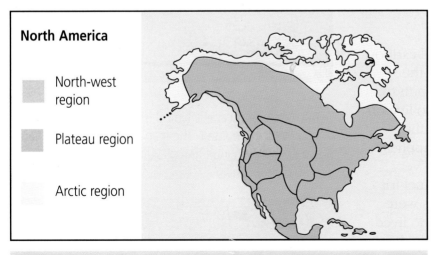

North America

North-west region

Plateau region

Arctic region

This map shows where each of the native people that we are studying in this book lived.

The Arctic is usually defined as the area north of the tree line where there is continuous **permafrost**. In summer, the sun melts the top few centimetres of soil and plants sprout up to enjoy the one or two months of long sunny days before the ice forms again and the winter darkness closes in. In December, the sun hardly appears at all. In this remote area live the Inuit. In the nineteenth century, there were about 20 different Inuit groups in North America, speaking several different dialects between them. Here we will look at the five main groups. These were called the Mackenzie, Copper, Central, Labrador and Caribou eskimos.

The Mackenzies, Coppers, Centrals and Labradors

The first four groups lived on the coasts, scattered over vast areas. They hunted sea mammals and a few other animals, and they fished. The hunters only left the coast for about two or three months, in the short Arctic summer, to head inland to hunt the caribou (a type of reindeer).

The Caribou Eskimos

The Caribou Eskimos hunted caribou all year, but in winter, when the caribou migrated from the north to the south, the eskimos had to live on fish and the few musk oxen they could hunt. The low food supplies meant that famine was often very close. In addition, a lack of fuel for their fires meant their homes were colder than of those Inuit who lived on the coast and used seal blubber for lighting, heating and cooking.

Source A

This Arctic landscape is typical of where many of the Inuit lived and hunted. The map opposite shows where five of the main Inuit groups were based.

Eskimo

The European name given to the Inuit.

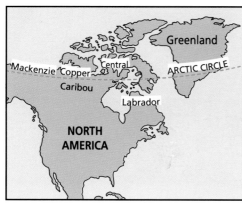

Things to do

1 How is the Arctic usually defined?

2 Why were the Caribou Inuit less well off than the coastal Inuit?

3 Look at Source A. What do you think it was like to live in this landscape?

The Inuit lived in the coldest inhabited land on earth. Even their houses were made of snow in the winter time. Sometimes these were made out of driftwood or the gigantic bones of whales covered in turf. But the Inuit who lived in the more central Arctic lands of Canada were experts at building domed snow houses where they lived from October to May when the warm summer sun began to melt their winter homes.

Building a snow house

The Inuit man would build a snow house by cutting blocks of snow and placing them in a circle around him. His helper passed the blocks to him until he had built up to the dome which he finished with a single, large block of snow. When this was done, he knelt down, cut a doorway and crawled out. Sometimes he added a tunnel to the door to cut down on heat loss. Round the inside of the walls the man built a ledge of snow blocks. Caribou furs covered the ledge on which the family sat and slept.

Inside a snow house

Once the family was inside and the blubber lamp was lit, the snow melted slightly. This was excellent because the incredibly low temperatures outside soon re-froze the snow, filling in all the cracks. Some families hung skins around the walls for added insulation. The temperature inside could rise as high as a comfortable 16°C, particularly if the wife was cooking. To provide ventilation the snow house had a windowpane made of stretched seal intestines. Cold air came in through the tunnel doorway and stale air went out through a small hole in the windowpane. At night, before the family went to sleep, the wife shortened the length of the flame in the soapstone lamp and filled the lamp bowl with crushed, frozen pieces of blubber. This small flame needed little oxygen, so the windowpane hole could be stuffed with dry grass. A large stone was placed at the tunnel entrance to stop the sledge dogs coming in to eat the meat supplies while everyone was asleep.

Source A

Building a small snow house. Inuit often built snow houses as temporary shelters while travelling.

Winter was a good time for socialising. Family and friends travelled by sledge to visit, sing, tell stories or dance. Often a family snow house was too small and some groups built communal snow houses.

This photograph shows the inside of a more permanent snow house. The woman in the picture is chewing skin to soften it.

Source C

An extract from a government report on the Inuit written in 1932.

Whatever the nature of their winter dwellings, all Inuit lit them with a stone lamp burning oil from the blubber of the sea mammals, or, in the case of the Inuit inland from Hudson Bay, the fat of the caribou. They used this lamp to cook their food, and made their cooking pots from the same material, soapstone, or in Alaska, pottery. Only during the summer months, from May to September, did they dispense with the lamp and cook outdoors with driftwood, or with the miserable fuels supplied by their treeless habitat – heather and dwarf willow.

Things to do

1 Describe how an Inuit man made a snow house.

2 Why was snow a good building block for winter houses?

3 How did the Inuit cook in winter and in summer?

4 Why do you think the winter was a good time for socialising?

The coastal Inuit hunted seal for most of the year. In the short Arctic summer they could hunt from boats. Sometimes they would harpoon the seals as they were swimming or catch them on the ice. However, by October the ice grew across the water and one clear frosty night would transform all open water into ice that could be walked on. This was a good time to hunt seal.

How the hunters caught seal

Seals are mammals and need to breathe, so they come up to a small hole in the ice at intervals. They have wonderful hearing and once snow has fallen, they can hear the crackle of a person walking above them from a long way away. But on ice they can be fooled. The hunter used to tie extra bearskin soles with the fur side out to his kamiks (shoes). He went out on the ice and stood motionless for a time, listening for a seal breathing in a hole nearby. The seals exhale (breathe out) and inhale (breathe in) six or seven times, and every time the hunter heard the bubbly sound of the seal breathing, he would take a step forward. When the seal swam away, the hunter stood still. This went on until the hunter was poised over the hole so that when the seal returned, the hunter could plunge his harpoon down into the seal's skull. Usually the animal was stunned or killed. The hunter would quickly enlarge the hole and drag the seal out. Later in the winter when the snow came, the wait was longer. Often, hunters sat quite still by a single breathing hole for hours.

Different types of seal

The most important seals for the Inuit living beyond the Arctic Circle were the three resident varieties that could be hunted all winter. These were the Walrus, the Bearded and the Ringed seals. Not only were these seals important for their meat and blubber, but also the Ringed seal in particular was food for the bears that made up part of the Inuit diet. Each of the three types of seal had different habits in winter.

The Walrus seal

The Walrus seal likes to stay near the coast but has to move further and further out to sea as the ice thickens. The seal can only knock a breathing hole in the ice if it is no more than about 10 to 12 centimetres thick.

Source A

This story was told to a young explorer called Vilhjalmur Stefansson when he was living with the Inuit on Victoria Island in 1910. (We will learn more about Stefansson in section 2.8.)

The Bearded seal

The man stood beside the seal hole watching for the seal to come up. When it did, it proved to be a Bearded one, but being a strong man he had been able to kill it. He had enlarged the breathing hole to pull the animal out. Now he looked round and saw that the other hunters were all far away, and he felt sure that none of them knew what kind of seal he had caught.

Deciding to cheat

He decided to pretend this was a small Ringed seal. He would keep the animal to himself and sell the skin to a neighbouring tribe who seldom caught Bearded seals. He cut the animal up and said he had killed a small seal. He pledged his wife to secrecy.

The story leaked out

But the story leaked out. People came to him and took away both the skin and the meat. He felt crushed by the disapproval of his people, but his punishment was to be made even heavier.

The worst punishment

Within a year he began to lose his eyesight and in another year he was completely blind. Since then he had been a charge upon the community. He said to me that while he was sure I was a good man, nevertheless to remember his story and pass it on warning others to avoid selfish ways.

The Bearded seal

The Bearded seal can come further in towards the coast under the ice because it has claws on its foreflippers that can keep open a breathing hole until the depth of ice is 20 to 25 centimetres. There are areas where the currents keep the ice fairly thin, despite hundreds of kilometres of sea ice further from the coast. These are favourite places for the Bearded seal who returns to them year after year. The Inuit knew all these places and relied on them for winter hunting.

The Ringed seal

The Ringed seal is the most common seal and hunts under the ice all winter, only coming up to its breathing holes or to areas of deep snow to sleep. This is rare. Generally the seals do most of their sleeping during the summer. They lie dozing on the ice floes and the Inuit of the coastal areas were adept at hours of patient hunting. They lay on the ice and imitated the shape and sleepiness of a seal. Since a seal slept for only about one minute before looking round, the hunter not only had to move slowly, but also had to imitate the sleeping and looking around movements of the seal, or the seal would not be fooled.

An Inuit seal hunter waiting by a breathing hole. He is holding his harpoon ready.

Things to do

1 How did the Inuit hunt seals in the summer?

2 Describe how the Inuit hunter fooled the seal in winter so that he could harpoon him.

3 Why were the resident varieties of seal important to the coastal Inuit?

4 Read Source A. What can we learn about the Inuit from this story?

Source A

An Inuit hunter. He has pushed his snow goggles on to his forehead while he uses the bow and arrow. The Inuit made snow goggles from bone, horn or wood. The narrow slits gave restricted vision but prevented snow blindness as the summer sun reflected off the snow.

Most Inuit made their home base in the areas where there was most food. This meant staying near the sea and close to the places where the sea mammals, particularly seals, were abundant. However, they moved inland at certain times of the year so that they could find wood, fish and other meat. They moved in small hunting groups.

How groups of hunters were formed

More often, these groups were made up of a few families if the men got on well and liked to hunt together. Also, if a young man wanted to marry a girl, he might join the family and hunt with the father for a year or two before marrying. But sometimes one family would hunt on their own. In a land where it required all their ingenuity to find food and shelter, there was no set form of government. Each family made their own decisions about where and when to hunt, and no area supported so many people that they could settle down for long. When midsummer was approaching, the hunters and their families would set off inland to hunt caribou.

Caribou

The Inuit liked caribou because it gave them a change in diet. Also caribou skins were excellent for making clothes. The hairs of the caribou are hollow. This makes the skins very light and warm, and they can be worn with the fur inwards. The hollow hairs prevent any damp sweatiness that could result in someone catching a chill as well as being uncomfortable in such a cold land.

Source B

This is a story from the explorer Vilhjalmur Stefansson about summer hunting in 1910.

Kirkpuk agrees to come hunting

We were to set off for Banks Island and engaged a man (Kirkpuk) we knew and liked, but in whom we had no great confidence. He had, however, an excellent wife. My companion Natkusiak and I were well able to hunt for food and raw material for clothing, but we needed an able woman to do sewing for us. I was surprised that Kirkpuk and his wife were willing to go with us, for they had a baby not more than six or eight weeks old, but they told me they would leave the child with its grandmother. It was necessary, Kirkpuk told us, that we should wait a day or two while his wife finished cutting up blubber and putting it in bags for the summer. Most of these he would give to his wife's father to cache on the mainland.

Kirkpuk changes his mind

Two days later the weather had changed but so, unfortunately, had Kirkpuk's mind. During the night he and his wife had had time to think of many things: how badly they would miss their baby and so on. And anyway, Kirkpuk now recollected he had promised so-and-so that he would meet him to hunt that summer at Bear Lake. I was a little unreasonably annoyed. There was nothing wrong about it from the Eskimo point of view. The relation of master and man is unknown. He had told me what he felt like doing at that particular moment. Now he had changed his mind and there was nothing to be done but inform me.

The best time to take the caribou skins was towards winter when the caribou was growing a new coat. The Inuit also collected the antlers and bones to make tools. The sinew made sewing thread and lines for sealing and fishing. Even the stomach contents were used, because the half-digested vegetation was rich in vitamins. The meat was cooked and eaten, and the marrow from the bones was a great delicacy.

Eating and storing food

Through the short Arctic summer and the autumn, other animals such as bears, wolves, musk oxen and birds of all sorts were hunted and eaten. In the spring, birds' eggs were collected. Hunting and collecting went on all the time. Sometimes there was plenty of food. But this meant there was often a problem storing it for the times when blizzards might keep a family indoors for days. One way to store food was in the ground. In most areas there was permafrost a few centimetres down even in summer. By digging into this, fish could be stored and dug up later – frozen. Another way to secure food was by covering it with heavy stones to deter wolves, bears and **wolverines** or by building a platform a couple of metres from the ground.

Things to do

1 Why did the coastal Inuit move inland at certain times of the year?

2 Read Source B.

   a Why was Stefansson annoyed with Kirkpuk?

   b How does he explain that this annoyance was unreasonable?

Source A

By November, in the Arctic Circle, the water has frozen into ice and the sun is far down on the horizon. This was a good time to start travelling, while there was still some light and the ice was firm enough to take the weight of dog sleds. There could be several reasons for travelling at this time. Men who had had a good hunting year and had plenty of food cached for the winter could afford the time to take their families to visit friends. A man who had not had a good year might need to visit friends and relatives so that his family were fed during the winter months. Dog sleds were used all winter until about May, when the snow and ice began to thaw. They were used for hunting in autumn and spring, and in calm times in the winter. After a good hunt, the sledges were piled with meat or skins, and driven home.

In open land or on ice, dogs could be harnessed so they fanned out and all pulled equally together. Among trees they had to be harnessed one behind the other.

How the sledges were made

If possible, men made their sledges from wood and used bone or antler for the runners. But if it was necessary, they would use anything they could find. Even if iron was available through trading, the skilled Inuit would often use mud to make the bottom surface of the runners for the sledges. They collected the

We remember an incident some years ago near Baffin Island. A family needed to travel and made a sledge from frozen caribou skins, crossbars of frozen meat and salmon planed down (carved into shape) with an axe, and off they went one day just as the sun had returned – a good time to start on a trip. The going was fine and everybody was even able to sit on the sleds unless the route took them up steep hills.

But one night when they all were asleep, the Föhn wind (a warm south-westerly wind) overtook them. They woke up to find the temperature had risen above freezing, and three of their sleds had thawed and disintegrated. As usual the dogs had been unharnessed during the night, and they had taken advantage of the feast. They ate not only the crossbars but also the sledge runners as well, and all the provisions for the trip. Those familiar with the appetite of an Eskimo dog know how soon they can finish everything in sight, even their harnesses. Snow soon fell and hunting was out of the question. The party ate their dogs and even their skin clothes. They were found almost dead themselves, in late spring.

mud in summer and stored it in round balls. In winter they took it into the houses to thaw and put it on the runners in a thick layer. When it was frozen, they pared it down with a knife until it was smooth, then applied a thin layer of lukewarm water using a piece of bearskin as a brush. The water froze into thin ice making a smooth runner that would glide over the snow.

The dogs

The dogs who pulled the sledges lived outside. In the summer they sprawled on the ground around the tents of their owners. In winter, they curled up close together with their noses tucked under their bushy tails. They were fierce animals who worked in a strict hierarchy (order of importance) under their leader. They could attack other dogs (and sometimes people) who came too close, but they were always obedient to their master and family. A good team of twelve dogs could pull a sledge of up to a half a tonne in weight and could travel at up to 32 kilometres an hour. How fast and how far they could go depended on the conditions. In November, the ice was rough and hard on their feet. Crossing the frozen sea meant the dogs travelled long distances on salt ice. It could be very painful if the salty water got between the dogs' toes and refroze. So the men would make small skin boots for them. Sometimes, older dogs would stop pulling the sledge, hold up a paw and refuse to move until a boot was tied on.

Things to do

1 Why was November a good time to start travelling?

2 List all the things that might be used to make a sledge.

3 Read Source B. Why did disaster strike the people on Baffin Island in February?

Inuit women were valued for their ability to make the tailored clothes necessary to withstand the Arctic climate. They also processed the meat and skins of animals that had been hunted, cooked the food, looked after children and participated in fishing. The men were the hunters, major food providers, and makers of tools and houses. When a man and woman married, both of them knew exactly what their jobs were and what they would be expected to do.

Inuit marriages and relationships

There was no ceremony for marriage, so either party could break up the union when they wanted. But once the couple had children they mostly stayed together, though not necessarily all the time. Spouse (husband and wife) exchange was part of a complicated system among some of the Inuit people. In a land where starvation was always a danger, a network of alliances was essential. Some of these were formed by linking namesakes, by singing partners (friends who sang together), by adoption and by spouse exchange where a couple might change partners for while. These exchanges worked very well in good times but carried with them obligations of food and shelter in bad times. Any children of the exchanges regarded each other as brothers and sisters whether there was any blood relationship or not, so the network of alliances continued.

Source A

Women and men of the Inuit each had their own jobs and talents. The men were expected to be able to make tools, for example. Here the man is using a bow drill.

Source B

Inside a large snow house. At night the only light was from small oil lamps. The oil came from the blubber, or fat, of seals. Women stored blubber in large bags for both eating and using as fuel.

Source C

An extract about children from a book giving details of the Arctic year, published in 1958.

The children who are always running in and out at all times of the day, now usually stop going to their mothers to be undressed and tucked down on the sleeping ledge beneath a pile of skins. Now in April, when the days are long, the children just lie down on the sledges and sleep. If it is only 25 or 30 degrees below freezing, their skin clothes are enough to keep them warm, and should they feel a little chilly, they have only to wake up and play again. Then, too, sometimes they lie down among the dogs. Since these dogs will kill a dog from another household who comes too close, it is amazing to see children who can hardly walk, stroll in among them, push some of the dogs to one side, and lie down to take a nap, ignoring the snarls and grumbling.

Things to do

1 List the different jobs that were done by the women and the men.

2 Look at Sources A and B. What evidence is there of the sort of skills men and women had?

3 Read Source C. What sort of freedom did Inuit children have?

4 Why was the network of alliances more important to the Inuit than it would be in Britain today?

Source A

People needed to be very clever to survive in a land with no wood and no metal to speak of. One example of this ingenuity was the kayak (a canoe that had a cover over the top of it). Further south, tribes covered their canoes with the bark of trees or, on the north-west coast, they cut the canoes from the tree trunks themselves. But in the Arctic, a man was lucky to find the driftwood to make the frame of his kayak. Then it was covered with seal skin. This was often done by his wife, and she might redo it each year to make sure there was a good waterproof covering.

The man is carrying a kayak across the ice. The kayaks were stored outside the snow houses all winter when they could not be used. In winter everyone hunted on the ice and travelled by dog sled.

Kayaks and umiaks: who used them

The kayak was used by one person whose waterproof sealskin jacket fastened over the hole to make himself and his kayak waterproof – even if he capsized. From the kayak, men hunted seal and other sea mammals, and fish. The kayak was stored away all winter when the sea was frozen over. A larger vessel used by the Inuit was the sea-going umiak. This could hold about ten people and was used for whaling. The umiak was made of driftwood and covered with walrus skins. It was propelled by both paddling and using a sail.

What happened when white men came to the Arctic

White people came to the Arctic in the nineteenth century so that they could hunt whales. This was often the first time the Inuit had seen white people, and the contact between the two didn't always work in the natives' favour. Unfortunately, white people 'carried' diseases such as smallpox, dysentery and even influenza. Because the Inuit had never been exposed to these diseases before, they had no immunity (no way that their body could fight the germs) against them. Sometimes, whole communities were almost wiped out. Also, the whites brought with them tea, sugar, flour and alcohol. The Inuit were not used to these 'new' foods, and often found them difficult to digest.

Working for the whites

In 1860, American whalers expanded whaling into Hudson Bay. The local Inuit got jobs as crew members on the boats that went out hunting whales. But instead of being paid for this work in money, they were paid in goods (things that were useful to them). For instance, if a hunter killed a whale, he might be given a wooden whaleboat.

The big whaling ships spent all winter in Hudson Bay and were frozen in by the ice. The Inuit built their villages on the ice by the ships, and went on board for meals, dances and other entertainment in the wooden 'house' built on the deck. In return, the Inuit supplied the ship's crew with fresh meat all winter. The last whaling ships left Hudson Bay in 1915, and the Inuit were sorry to see them go.

Source B

An extract from a book in which Leah Arnaujaq, who worked for the white whalers, says how the Inuit felt when the whalers left.

We wondered, but we never really knew, why the whalers didn't come back. We were kind of regretful because we remembered how good their food had tasted and we remembered everybody getting together like a big family. When the whalers left, that big family feeling was gone.

Hudson's Bay Company

- Hudson Bay is the large bay in northern Canada. When explorers first sailed into Hudson Bay they thought they had found the north-west sea passage to the Pacific Ocean and to Asia. The Hudson's Bay Company was founded in England in 1760 both to keep looking for a sea passage to the Pacific and to trade in the area, particularly in furs. The Company still exists today.

Things to do

1 What is a kayak?

2 How was a kayak made?

3 What was an umiak used for?

4 Read Source B. Why was the author regretful?

5 What were the advantages and disadvantages of contact with white people?

Source A

Vilhjalmur Stefansson describes some of his experiences when he met Inuit who had never met white people.

The meeting

When we approached the village every man, woman and child was outdoors, waiting for us excitedly, for they could tell from afar that we were no ordinary visitors. The man whom we had first approached explained to an eagerly silent crowd that we were friends from a distance who had come without evil intent and immediately the whole crowd (about 40 people) came running towards us. As each came up he would say: 'I am So-and-so. I am well disposed. I have no knife. Who are you?' After being told our names in return and being assured that our knives were packed away in the sledge, each would express satisfaction. Sometimes a man would present his wife, or a woman her husband, according to which came up first. The women were in more hurry to be presented, for they must, they said, go back to their houses to cook us something to eat.

Building the house

After the women had gone, the men asked us whether we preferred to have our camp right in the village or a little outside it. On talking it over we agreed that it would be better to camp about 200 yards from the other houses, so as to keep our dogs from fighting with theirs. When this was decided, half a dozen small boys were sent home to get their fathers' snow-knives and house-building mittens so the best house-builders could set about erecting for us the house in which we were to live as long as we cared to stay with them. When it was finished and furnished with skins, lamps and the other things that go to make a snow-house the cosiest of camps, they told us they hoped we would stay for a long while. It was to be a holiday, they said, for this was the first time their people had been visited by strangers from so great a distance that even their country was unknown. These well bred and hospitable people were the savages we had come so far to see.

Speaking their language

The dialect they spoke differed so little from the Mackenzie River speech, which I had acquired in three years of living in the houses and camps of the western Eskimos, that I could make myself understood from the first. It cannot have happened often in the history of the world that the first white man to visit a primitive people was one who spoke their language. Long before the year was over I became one of them, and even from the first hour we were able to converse sympathetically on subjects of common concern.

Source B

An Inuit woman and child.

Invited to dinner

Before the house was quite ready, children came running from the village to announce that their mothers had cooked dinner. The houses were so small that it was not convenient to invite all three of us into the same one to eat; besides, it was not etiquette to do so, as we now know. My host was the seal hunter whom we had first approached on the ice. His house would, he said, be a fitting one in which to offer me my first meal among them, for his wife's people came from very far to the west. She would therefore like to ask me questions.

Food and conversation

It turned out, however, that his wife was not a talkative person but motherly and hospitable. She had boiled some seal meat for me, but she had not boiled any fat, for she did not know whether I preferred the blubber boiled or raw. They always cut it in small pieces and ate it raw themselves; but the pot still hung over the lamp, and anything she put into it would be cooked in a moment.

When I told her that my tastes quite coincided with theirs – as, in fact, they did – she was delighted. People were much alike, then, after all, though they came from a great distance. My hostess picked out for me the lower joint of a seal's foreleg and handed it to me, along with her own copper-bladed knife. After I had eaten my fill of fresh seal meat and drunk two pint cupfuls of blood-soup, my host and I moved farther back on the bed-platform where we could sit comfortably, propped up against bundles of soft caribou skins and talk.

Vilhjalmur Stefansson was an American Arctic explorer for several years. He learnt to speak the Mackenzie dialect of the Inuit language. He also learnt to hunt and live in the same way as the Inuit (although he used matches to light fires and a rifle for hunting). In 1910, he met the Inuit who lived in the area around the Dolphin and Union Strait. They had never seen a white person before.

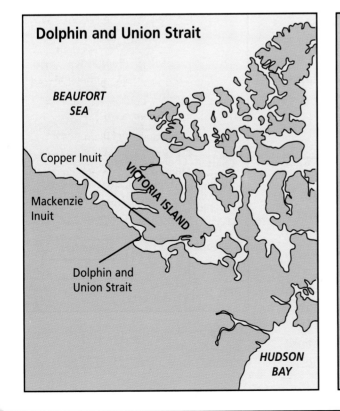

Dolphin and Union Strait

BEAUFORT SEA

Copper Inuit

VICTORIA ISLAND

Mackenzie Inuit

Dolphin and Union Strait

HUDSON BAY

Things to do

1 Read Source A.

   a How many people lived in the village?

   b What food was Stefansson offered?

   c What evidence is there for Stefansson's comment that the Inuit were well bred and hospitable people?

   d What difference does it make to Stefansson's meeting with the Inuit that he can speak their language?

2 What can you tell about the Inuit around the Dolphin and Union Strait from Stefansson's account?

3.1 FAR FROM THE EDGE: THE PEOPLE OF THE NORTH-WEST COAST

The native peoples of the north-west coast lived in a land with a mild climate, where the trees grew lush and tall, on a coastal strip backed by high snow-capped mountains on one side and small rocky bays on the other. With an annual rainfall of about 300 centimetres, it rained on most days. The sound of rushing water could be heard everywhere as streams and rivers tumbled on their way to the sea. This was a very different land from the frozen Arctic where the Inuit lived.

How the people of the north-west coast lived

Most people of the north-west coast lived in two villages – a summer one and a winter one. Their summer houses were simple brush or wooden shelters by the rivers where they went fishing. They caught salmon by the hundred and what they did not need to eat immediately, they dried on racks in the sun for winter stores.

The winter houses were more substantial. They were situated in sheltered sites within easy reach of the beaches so that people could travel from village to village to visit. A village could have 30 or more wooden plank houses. Anywhere from 12 to 100 people lived in a single multi-family dwelling. The large stores of dried fish and berries meant there was plenty of food throughout the winter. Also, the largest house in the village, belonging to the chief, was ideal for ceremonies. With plenty of stored food and leisure, winter was a time for socialising.

Rank and wealth

No other North American peoples put such a high value on rank and wealth. The family into which a person was born largely determined their rights, duties and privileges from birth to death. This included everything from the rights to fishing grounds, to marriage contracts. Families were related according to kinship. In the north this kinship came through the mother's side. A man's heir was not his son; his heir was his sister's son. In the south it was more usual for kinship to come through the father.

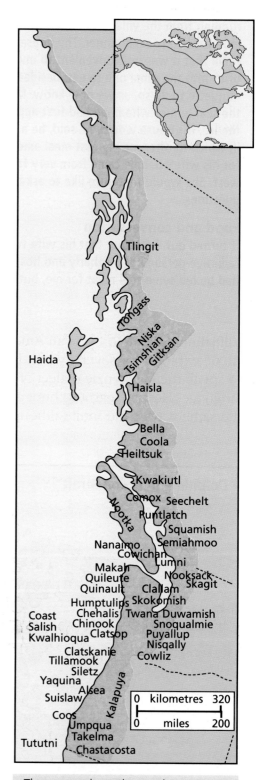

The areas where the north-west coast tribes lived.

Relatives and clans

As well as blood relations there were also clans (larger groupings, similar to a very extended family). Among the large tribe of the Tlingit, in the north, there were two clans. They were called the Raven and the Wolf. Among another tribe, called the Tsimshian there were four clans – Raven, Wolf, Eagle and Whale. All clan members had to marry outside their clan. If a member of the Wolf Clan of the Tlingit people was travelling far from home and got into difficulties (became ill, lost all his belongings, was attacked, etc) he would ask for help from any member of the Wolf Clan in another tribe up and down the coast. Not only were there divisions such as clans (and even sub-clans) but also there were divisions or classes in each village. All this led to a complicated class structure – but one where everyone knew their place.

Source A

The structure of a typical village.

- Each village had a *head chief* who inherited his position (through his mother or his father).

- The head chief was the highest-ranking member of the most important family. He was usually the wealthiest man, and was expected to hold feasts and to help the poor, the orphaned and the old.

- Each clan also had a *clan chief*.

- Each household had a *household chief*.

- The relatives of the chiefs often formed a class of their own, sometimes called *nobles*.

- Most other people were *commoners*, owing allegiance to the various chiefs.

- A special group were the *shamans*, who were doctors both for the physical body and the spirit.

- At the very bottom of the scale were the *slaves*. These had usually been captured in raiding parties or born to slaves in the village.

Things to do

1 Describe the land of the north-west coast peoples.

2 Look at the map. As far as you can tell, which tribes were likely to do as much sea fishing as river fishing?

3 Look at Source A.

   a Who was the most important man in the village?

   b Write a short paragraph about the class structure in the village.

4 What made it possible for the north-west coast people to hold ceremonies and visit each other during the winter?

5 What was the advantage of belonging to a clan?

The people of the north-west coast did not develop skills in farming. There was no need. They were able to live comfortably by fishing, hunting and gathering.

Hunting and collecting food

Food collection started seriously in the spring. The chiefs owned the hunting lands. When the new season began, each chief held a meeting of his group and reminded everyone that the hunting area was his. Then he generously offered it to the people to use. His offer reflected the greatness of his status and the first animals caught or plants gathered always went to the chief. When they were collected, the chief invited the whole village to a feast.

River fish

Every spring, the salmon swam up river from the sea, to spawn. Sometimes there were so many that they spilled on to the banks on either side. This was a great time for fishermen. Since the salmon did not eat when they were going to spawn there was no point in using hook and bait. The fishermen either used spears or built traps and nets. The skeleton of the first fish caught in each river was put back into the river to be carried out to sea to ensure that the salmon came back again next year. After this **ritual**, the men caught as many fish as they could. They took them home and the women immediately cleaned the catch. Fresh salmon were eaten every day during the spring. The remainder were slit into strips. These strips were hung on racks to be dried in the sun or smoked and stored for the winter.

Salmon were not the only fish available in this area. The eulachon also swam upstream to spawn in the spring and summer. White settlers called this the candle fish, because it was so oily that when fitted with a wick (a length of thread or string) it could be burnt like a candle. However, the fish was also tasty when cooked, and the oil from it was used for cooking and seasoning other dishes.

Fishing at sea

The skills of the fishermen were tested even more at sea. Halibut, herring, flounder, sardines and sturgeon were all caught. Going further afield, men hunted seals on the offshore islands, sea otters (mostly for their fur) and sealions. Only a few tribes, such as the Nootka, prided themselves on being whalers.

Source A

Captain Lewis writing about the tiny eulachon, or candle, fish in his diary on 24 February 1806. (Captain Lewis and Captain Clark led the first expedition by the US government to reach the Pacific coast of North America.)

I find them best when cooked in Indian style which is by roasting a number of them together on a wooden spit. They are so fat they require no additional sauce, and I think them superior to any fish I ever tasted.

Source B

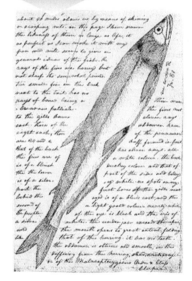

A page from Lewis's diary showing the candle fish.

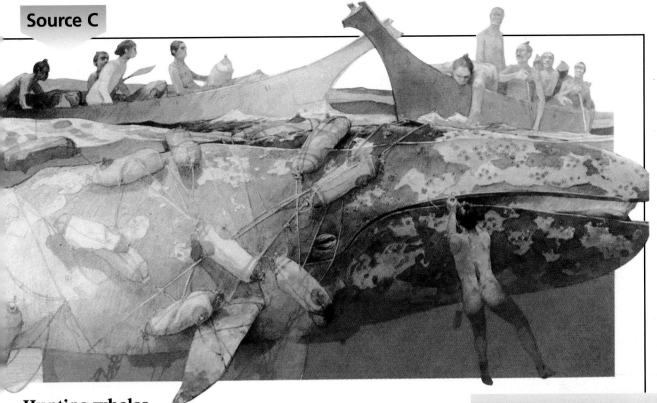

A modern drawing of a whale hunt. The sealskin floats are to stop the dead whale from sinking.

Hunting whales

Hunting whales was difficult and dangerous, and whalers had high status in their villages. A whaling leader usually inherited his position but he did not keep it unless he was expert. Before a hunt, rituals concentrated the minds of the men about to set out. They meditated and prayed, and they sang songs. When the men set out it was in ten-metre long cedar canoes. At least three canoes (and often as many as ten) were needed to hunt the whales using harpoons with sealskin floats attached. When near enough, the harpoonist launched the harpoon as near to the whale's head as possible, to keep the canoe from being wrecked by the lashing tail. With the harpoon stuck in the flesh and secured to the men in the canoe by a long line, the chase was on as the whale swam away to rid himself of the men. Sometimes he dived, but the line held and after hours (or often longer) the whale died and the floats kept the body from sinking. The whale meat was divided among the village according to each family's rank. The best pieces of whale blubber went to the man who had secured the first harpoon.

Gathering other foods

Although whale-hunting was exciting, dangerous and high **status**, much of the day-to-day food – such as fruits, berries and roots – was gathered quietly from the forests. In addition to these, shellfish were gathered from the sea shore. This gathering was done by women and children. The women dried or smoked many of the foods to preserve them for the winter.

Things to do

1 Who owned the hunting lands?

2 Why were salmon so important to the north-west coast people?

3 How did the men set about a whale hunt?

Source A

A house interior.

Wood was plentiful. So many of the people of this area built substantial plank houses in which they lived for most of the year. Some of these houses were as long as 100 metres and as wide as 20 metres.

How houses were constructed

The houses had two parts. One was the inner framework of cedar logs that was permanent. The framework was then covered with cedar planks. The roof planks rested on the roof framework, while the walls were made by laying planks on edge on top of each other to rest against the inner framework. Most of the planks were lashed to the framework, though a few might be left loose on the roof to make an adjustable smoke hole. Sometimes there were gaps in the wall planks for windows and always a gap in the end wall for a door. The windows could be covered with cedar bark mats to keep the rain out. The planks could easily be taken off and carried to a new location to be put up around another frame.

Who lived in the houses?

The big houses contained many families. Each family had all the space between two posts of the inner framework across to the middle of the house. The family shared a central fire with the family opposite. There were sleeping benches along the walls, and each family section was marked off with a cedar mat curtain or a plank.

Of course, not every house was like this. Some were smaller, perhaps holding only four families who all shared one common fire place. Some had gabled or pointed roofs, some had large flat, gently sloping roofs, which were good for ceremonies and dances. Some had vertical wall planks instead of horizontal.

Winter and summer homes

These were often built on the coast, close to the beach. From there people could visit other settlements by canoe. In the summer, most people left the wooden houses and set off for the fishing grounds or hunting grounds where they camped and gathered the food they needed. However, most north-west coast people lived in wooden houses for the winter.

Source B

An adaptation from a book written by an explorer called Meares, when he visited a house on the north-west coast of America in the 1790s.

When we went into the house, we were very surprised at the vast area it enclosed. It contained a large square, boarded up close on all sides to the height of 20 feet, with planks that were uneven in size. Three enormous trees, carved and painted, formed the rafters, which were supported at the ends and in the middle by massive images, carved out of huge blocks of timber. The same kind of broad planks covered the whole building to keep out the rain. But they could also be removed so that fresh air and light would come in to the building, and smoke could be let out. In the middle of this big room were several fires.

The trees that supported the roof were so big they could make the most sturdy man-of-war look small. The door by which we entered was the mouth of one of these huge images, which, large as it was, did not overpower the other features of this monstrous vision. We climbed up a few steps on the outside and climbed down the chin into the house, where we found other things that surprised us – the number of men, women and children who made up the family of the chief. It consisted of at least 800 persons.

Things to do

Look at Source A and read Source B.

1 How does the information in Source B help you to understand what the house of a native of the north-west coast was like?

2 In what ways was the house described by Meares similar and in what ways was it different from the house in the photograph?

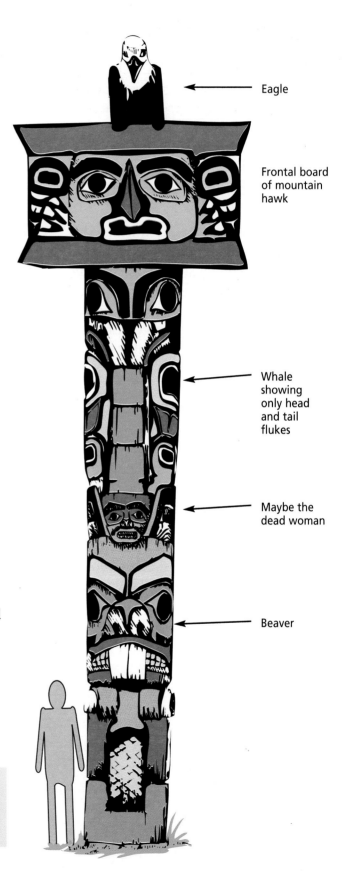

Eagle

Frontal board of mountain hawk

Whale showing only head and tail flukes

Maybe the dead woman

Beaver

A totem pole is the popular name given to the poles that were erected outside houses. These poles were carved from a single red cedar tree trunk. The carvings represented the history of the family, often going back to their mythical beginnings.

The function of totem poles

This varied with different peoples along the coast. But overall, they were historical monuments displaying the origins, exploits, achievements, acquisitions and supernatural experiences of the person or family. They proclaimed wealth and status in the village and in the tribal group. A number of explorers and traders who visited the area in the eighteenth century commented on the use of carved poles as part of the structure and entrance to a house. However, these comments were generally about houses that belonged to a distinguished noble or chief.

Totem poles linked to explorers and traders

Later, free-standing poles began to appear. These are linked to the arrival of white fur traders. The demand for furs, such as sea otter pelts, was very high and brought wealth to the people of the north-west coast. The increased wealth was displayed in the carvings on poles, which became more elaborate. This creativity reached its peak in the 1860s.

A Haida Mortuary Pole. The box behind the frontal board contained the cremated remains of a high-ranking Haida woman.

After this, the decline in the number of sea otters, inter-tribal wars and devastating European diseases such as smallpox (which were 'carried' to the area with explorers and traders) began to reduce the native population. All of these things began to affect the wealth of the area.

How poles are read

A totem pole should be read from the top to the bottom. The top figure may identify the owner through his crest – perhaps Raven, Eagle, Killer Whale or Thunderbird. The largest figure, often at the base of the pole, is the most important in the story. Small figures of people or animals have meaning, too, but interpretation of old poles is often impossible if no other documents exist. For instance, a man might have had a pole carved and included a carving of the crest of a man who had injured him. There is now no way of knowing this story.

Things to do

1 What sort of poles did the explorers and traders see in the eighteenth century?

2 **a** Why was there a boom in totem pole building in the nineteenth century and why did it decline?

   b Why do you think greater wealth from the hunting of furs might bring more inter-tribal wars?

3 Why is it often impossible to know the meaning of all the carvings on a totem pole? What does this tell you about the type of culture of the north-west coast people?

There are many mythical, supernatural beings that have become the crests of the various cultures of the north-west coast peoples. These crests include: Raven, Bear, Killer Whale, Eagle, Split-Person, Fog-Woman and hosts of others. Many of them have their origins in the ancient myth time before the world was as it is now. This was a time when humans and animals were not separate, when they could transform from one to the other – and often did.

Inheriting a crest

A family came to own its crest through an ancestor who had an encounter with a supernatural creature. The family then had the right to use that creature's likeness on totem poles, house fronts, carved boxes, dishes, masks and any property they had. If a song or dance had come out of the encounter, the family owned that too and no one else could perform it.

Acquiring a crest

Apart from inheriting the crest, a person could acquire it through marriage, conquering an enemy, trading, a gift for a special service or merely taking it over when a family died out. The crest was very much a piece of property.

Legends

Legends are traditional stories and many of the legends of the north-west coast people appear carved on totem poles, particularly if they relate to the family's crest. Although the legends vary throughout the region, and even from village to village, the basics remain the same.

The story of Fog-Woman *(the legend of how the salmon came to the rivers)*

Raven and his two slaves were fishing but caught only bullhead fish. When fog came up, they began paddling back to the camp; suddenly a young woman appeared in the canoe. She was Fog-Woman, the daughter of Chief Fog on the Salmon. Raven married her.

Fog-Woman was skilled at basket making and made a finely woven, watertight basket of spruce root. Raven complimented her on it. 'Watch what it can do,' she said. She dipped her hands into the fresh water in the

Source A

The best known legend, with many variations, is 'How Raven Stole the Sun'. It is recounted here.

There was a time when all the world was in darkness because a greedy chief kept the Sun, the Moon and the Stars in three wooden boxes in his house. He would occasionally lift the lid and let the light spill out. Hearing about the boxes, Raven was determined to bring daylight to the world and the wily old bird devised a plan.

Knowing that the chief's daughter went to the stream for water every day, Raven transformed himself into a hemlock needle and floated down the stream. When the young woman filled her box with fresh, cool water, he slid into the box and was carried to the house. The chief's daughter drank the water and swallowed the needle, and as a result, became pregnant. Eventually she gave birth to a dark, beady-eyed child. He cried a lot, mostly for the box with the bright, shiny ball inside, but the chief refused to allow him to play with it. Daily the child wheedled and whined, until the chief could stand it no more and allowed his grandson to play with the ball – just this once.

Seizing the opportunity, Raven transformed himself back into bird form, picked up the ball in his beak, and in a flash of black feathers, flew up and out through the smoke hole of the chief's house. Higher and higher he flew, spreading light all around the world for everyone to enjoy. Then he flung the shining globe into the sky, and there it remains to this day.

basket and brought out a large salmon. Daily, Fog-Woman dipped her hands in the basket and, daily, she fished out a salmon. Soon the fish-drying rack was hung with rows and rows of dried and smoked salmon, and the storehouse was full.

Raven boasted about all the salmon he had and this annoyed his wife. They quarrelled fiercely and eventually, Raven hit Fog-Woman with a dried salmon. She ran out of the house and down to the beach, followed by her husband who reached out to grab her. But as he did so, she turned into fog. Then all the dried and smoked salmon left the storehouse and the racks, and followed her into the sea – leaving Raven holding a useless bullhead.

Nowadays, it is Fog-Woman's daughter, Creek-Woman, who lives at the head of every stream, and it is she who brings the salmon back up the streams from the sea every year.

Totem poles are still carved today. Some are replacements for old ones that are decaying. Some are new ones.

Things to do

1 How did a family come to own its crest?

2 What sort of things could be owned as well as crests?

3 Apart from inheritance, how else could a person acquire a crest?

4 Read Source A. What things would you include on a totem pole to illustrate the story of 'How Raven Stole the Sun'. Make a drawing of your pole.

This totem pole was carved in 1981 to commemorate the Tlingit people of the Tongass area. It tells the legend of how the first salmon came to the rivers. It is at a heritage centre in Alaska.

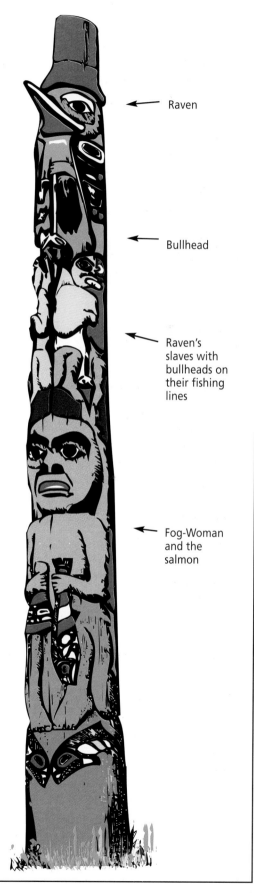

← Raven

← Bullhead

← Raven's slaves with bullheads on their fishing lines

← Fog-Woman and the salmon

Source A

A painting of a potlatch in 1859.

The totem poles, myths and legends were part of the unwritten history of the people of the north-west coast. Another way in which they kept alive and passed on their history was by speech-making, dancing and songs. Often this happened at a potlatch.

The origins and purpose of potlatches

Potlatch comes from the word 'pa-chitle' in the language of the Nuu-chah-nulth (Nootka). It means 'to give'. A potlatch was a huge party where the chief who was hosting it gave away hundreds of gifts to his guests. The purpose of the potlatch was to keep or gain prestige. But the potlatch might also be held for other reasons – for example, to celebrate the coming of age of a son or daughter, the raising of a new totem pole, in memory of an old chief, or to celebrate and affirm the new chief. Whatever the reason, the party could last for days.

Arriving at a potlatch

The guests would turn up from other villages by canoe, dressed in their finest clothes. Although they had come from as far away as 150 or so kilometres, they waited until they could step from their canoes on to land in their order of rank. The size of canoes was significant. The greater the chief, the larger his canoe and the more people he came with. Some guests brought their slaves with them to paddle their canoes.

What happened at the potlatch

Once ashore, the guests then mingled with each other to retell old stories, learn the latest news and enjoy lots of food. Apart from feasting and present-giving, there was dancing, singing and speeches. This was the core of the potlatch: to witness the host laying claim to certain privileges and rights in song, dance, speech and even works of art such as totem poles.

In a culture with no written history, this was the way in which events were recorded and passed on.

If a totem pole was going to be raised, the guests sat in order of rank as the pole was unveiled. They all helped to hoist the pole with ropes, then listened to the speech, which was usually illustrated with dances and song. While this was happening, the host and his relatives listened to admiring remarks from the guests. Any insulting remarks could lead to future war.

At the end of the potlatch came the gift giving. For months the host had been gathering together presents. They were given out according to rank.

The benefits of potlatches

Potlatches helped to encourage the trade of the area. One of the most prized gifts were the Chilkat blankets. These were woven by Tlingit women from the **fleece** of mountain goats. A chief would buy as many as possible to give as presents, together with fur robes of bearskin, sea otter, mink and deer skin. The most highly prized gifts were coppers. These were pieces of copper about one metre high, often engraved with the owner's crest. Since these were so highly prized, a host might give only one away or even break one and give the pieces to a rival chief. The rival then had to break a copper of even greater value or be shamed.

By the standards of any hunter-gatherer society, the people of the north-west coast were wealthy and became more so when white fur traders bought as many furs as the native people could trap. So, by the middle of the nineteenth century there were more potlatches than ever. More presents were given and more goods were destroyed to show wealth. In 1884, the Canadian government forbade potlatches, saying that they were wasteful. This ban remained in force until 1951.

Source B

A Chilkat robe to wear at a potlatch.

Things to do

1 What is a potlatch?

2 Look at Source A.

  a What present is being given here?

  b What evidence is there of contact with non-Native American culture?

3 What other reasons might the Canadian government have had for banning potlatches in 1884?

Potlatches were not the only gatherings that the peoples of the north-west coast attended. In winter, they felt that the spirit world was very close to them. They met together around the fire in the big log houses. There, in the flickering firelight, they watched the dances and listened to the songs of the winter ceremonies. They felt that the world of the spirits, of animals and people were all one.

The shamans

The most powerful spirit of all was believed to belong to the medicine people, or shamans. This was an unsought spirit that could take possession of women as well as men. Anyone who possessed it was both honoured and feared. Often the position of shaman in a village was inherited through either the mother or the father. But sometimes new shamans appeared. If a child seemed to have the right qualities, parents might take him or her to the village shaman and, if chosen, the parents would pay for the child to become the shaman's apprentice. Some shamans specialised in healing, some in retrieving lost

Source A

Many of the masks and costumes used at gatherings represented the way in which animals, people or spirits could change into each other. The wooden masks were often made to open and reveal either the dancer or another face inside.

Source B

A winter ceremony.

souls, others were believed to be able to bring about events such as success in war, and a war party would not leave without getting the blessing of a shaman.

Illnesses and cures

Families used medicinal herbs to treat illness and only called in the shaman when their efforts had failed. The cause of unknown illness was often thought to be an object that was sent into the sick person's body by a person or spirit who was angry with him or her. The shaman had to find this and remove it. This might be done by using a sucking tube (a long bone or wooden tube) and acting out the removal. It was important that the relatives of the sick person were there to witness and partake of the ritual.

Retrieving lost souls

To retrieve a lost soul, shamans often went on pretend journeys to the land of the dead. These journeys varied from tribe to tribe. They might involve trances, where the shaman worked him or herself into a frenzy. Or they might involve acting out the journey by land and sea. Another way to bring back a soul was to use a soul catcher, which might be made out of bone. Perhaps, nowadays, we would see this loss of the soul as a mental illness.

Herbal medicines

Like many so-called primitive people, the women and men who inhabited the north-west coast knew a great deal about the medicinal properties of the plants in their own area. Most shamans were skilled herbalists, but many ordinary people also used herbs for everyday problems such as cuts and sores. The Haida used the bark of the lodgepole pine as a cast for broken bones, while its sap was heated and used

for sore joints. The Bella Coola used cherry bark to bind wounds and the inner bark of cedar was used as tourniquets. Like many other peoples around the world, they used spiders' webs to put across wounds as a mesh to stop bleeding and aid healing. Also, a type of cabbage was used as a poultice on inflamed joints. Hot water was poured on dandelion roots to make a tea to treat stomach pain, and juniper was used as a cough medicine.

Source C

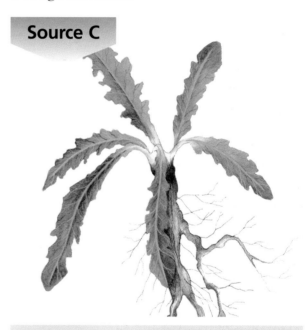

For hundreds of years dandelion root has been used by Europeans, Chinese, Indians and Native Americans, as a herbal treatment for the digestive system.

Things to do

1 What was special about a shaman?

2 In what types of job did shamans specialise?

3 What herbs did ordinary people use?

4 How do you think a knowledge of herbs was passed on from generation to generation?

Marriage was a contract between two people and their families. Negotiations began when the bridegroom's family spoke to the girl's family. This was followed by a feast where the boy's family praised his virtues and told the family's history. They also gave gifts known as the bride price. Among the Nootka it was customary to refuse the bride price three times. The higher the family's status the more the refusals.

Marriage ritual among the tribes

When a Kwakiutl bride and groom married, the bride's father gave certain property and honours to his son-in-law. These were not usually handed over until the first child was born at the earliest. The handing over meant the contract would end or it could be renewed (by the giving of more gifts to the bride's father). Getting married was complicated and involved much ritual. Divorce

Source A

A young girl. Her future husband's family would try to impress her family and give them gifts.

was simple. Either the husband or wife moved out of the home. If this was done in a friendly way, there was no more to be said. But there could be a great deal of trouble if either family felt insulted.

Among the Tlingit, where women held major positions in the tribal ranking, a wealthy woman sometimes chose to have several husbands. In other areas, it tended to be wealthy chiefs who had several wives.

How husbands and wives divided their tasks

Once married, the wife and husband divided the tasks each of them had to do. The women collected firewood. They gathered berries, roots and fruit from the forest, and shellfish and seaweed

Some of the earliest things that the north-west coast people liked to buy from white traders were metal tools. This chest is an example of what they could make with these tools.

Cooking

Cooking was a skilled job and was usually done by using hot stones. Smooth stones of various sizes were part of every woman's cooking equipment. She put them in the fire. When they were hot, she lifted them out with sticks, dipped them in water to wash off the ashes, then dropped them into her cooking box which was partly filled with water. The cooking box might be a wooden box, a tightly woven basket or a hollowed-out log. The stones were hot enough to make the water boil. An open work basket full of raw food was placed in the boiling water and more red hot stones were packed around it. Fish, meat and vegetables could be cooked like this. Food could also be baked on hot stones or steamed in closed pits.

from the beaches. They often carried home the animals the men had killed, then prepared, cooked and preserved the meat. They tanned the skins for clothes which they made. They also wove baskets and hats, and looked after the children.

The men hunted and fished, and made tools and wooden goods (from houses and canoes to cooking boxes and spoons). Men's skill was more concerned with providing the food, and this required tools from spears to canoes. The very best and biggest ocean-going canoes were made by special carpenters, but most men made their own smaller family canoe for local travelling. Women liked to use them for inshore fishing and visiting. The canoes were made from hollowed out logs of cedar trees, and the hollowing out took a long time using only fire and stone tools.

Things to do

1 Make a list of the women's tasks and the men's tasks within the family.

2 Look at Source B. How else do you think metal would change the lives of the people of the north-west coast. List as many things as you can.

3 How was food cooked?

Source A

The Nez Perce and the other Plateau tribes had their own traditional fishing grounds on the main rivers. They speared fish and also trapped them in basketwork traps. Once the fish were in the traps, they used clubs to kill them.

The Nez Perce were one of a number of tribes who lived on the land called the Plateau, between the north-west coast tribes and the Plains tribes to the east. For thousands of years they had lived by hunting such animals as elk, deer and mountain goat, beaver and otter. They gathered berries and other fruits, and nuts and **camas** bulbs which were a sweet, nutritious food. Above all they fished in the rivers in similar ways to the fishing of the north-west coast tribes. Salmon were plentiful.

Trading between the tribes

The different tribes each produced their own specialist (unique) goods. They met together in the autumn to trade. Mostly they travelled by canoe, navigating the dangerous rapids and waterfalls on the rivers, to meet together at places such as Dalles and Kettle Falls.

What goods were traded

Dentalium shells (much prized as decoration) came from the coast to be traded for such things as buffalo skins and camas bulbs. By the time the explorers Lewis and Clark met the Plateau tribes in 1806, white people's goods were a big feature of the trading. These included copper and brass kettles, old muskets, coffee pots, blankets, knives and brass wire.

Why the Nez Perce were different from other tribes

What set the Nez Perce apart initially was the horse. The Spanish introduced the horse into Mexico when they arrived in the sixteenth century. Over the years, some escaped into the wild and some were stolen. By the eighteenth century, the horse was widely used by the Native Americans and it changed their lives. Suddenly they had an animal that could travel fast and carry loads either by pulling the **travois** used by the Plains Indians or on its back. The tribes who used the horse became far more mobile. They could have bigger tipis because the horse could pull more than the dog, and they could hunt more successfully because they could pursue the buffalo and other game on horseback.

The Nez Perce were keen horsemen. Many of them spent the winter on the Plateau. In the summer, they made the long ride down to the Plains to hunt buffalo and live in tipis until autumn.

The Plateau lands were good for horses. The mountains and rivers prevented horses from straying too far and from being stolen. The well-watered valleys grew excellent grass for the horses to eat and gave them shelter in winter.

By the nineteenth century, the Nez Perce were no longer known for their canoes but for their horses. Lewis and Clark met and stayed with a number of Plateau tribes, including the Nez Perce, and were very impressed by the numbers of horses owned by different families. In particular they were impressed by the quality of the Nez Perce horses. They were also impressed by the Nez Perce themselves.

Trading fairs

Two tribes, the Wishram and the Wasco, usually hosted these fairs. They were the middlemen between the tribes of the north-west coast and the tribes of the Plateau.

Source B

Extract from a book about Lewis's and Clark's expedition during which they came across the Nez Perce tribe.

They are among the most amiable men we have seen. Their character is placid and gentle, rarely moved into passion.

Things to do

1 What food did the Nez Perce live on before they used horses to go hunting?

2 Who introduced the horse to North America?

3 What difference did the horse make to the Native Americans?

4 Why didn't the Inuit and the people of the north-west coast use horses?

The gentleness of the Nez Perce did not prevent them fighting when they had to. Once they owned horses they travelled further and more often. They frequently went to trading meetings at such places as the Dalles (see section 4.1), and they carried as many goods as they could on their horses to trade. Furthermore, in springtime they travelled eastward on horseback, through the mountain passes with laden horses, to trade with the Plains tribes and to hunt the buffalo themselves.

Types of goods that were traded

The trade goods that the Nez Perce took to the Plains were things like dried fish, salmon oil, cakes of camas and berries, hemp and hemp twine, pipes of green soapstone, eagle tail feathers, horn spoons, woven bags and dentalium shells bought from the tribes living on the Pacific coast.

One of the goods they were most famous for was a bow made from the horn of the mountain sheep. Pieces of horn were boiled until they were pliable. Then they were fixed together with salmon skin glue and bound with sinew. This made a bow tougher and more flexible than any other type of bow. It was in great demand among the Plains' tribes and might even cost as much as one horse.

The bow was used in hunting, but it was also used in warfare. While the Plains tribes liked to buy the Nez Perce bows and horses, the Nez Perce were keen to buy buffalo skin robes (the best of which were made by the Crow) and head-dresses (the best of which were made by the Sioux). Apart from these goods, the Nez Perce returned to the Plateau at the end of the summer with their horses loaded with buffalo skins and buffalo meat.

The Nez Perce at war

From early in the eighteenth century, the balance of the tribes was changed by three things – the horse, the arrival of white people in the east and the fact that the white people brought guns with them. In about 1750, the Blackfoot tribe bought guns from the Hudson's Bay Company and, with their superior fire power, they drove the Shoshoni and Flathead tribes back to the high Plateau. The Nez Perce allied themselves with these tribes and some desperate wars followed as they were drawn into Plains style warfare which involved scalp hunting and horse raiding.

Plains style warfare

As the Nez Perce became more nomadic, they took on the ways of the nomadic Plains tribes. Possessions are a hindrance if you are always on the move. Therefore, things such as honour in battle were more important for a man's status among the Plains tribes than how many goods he had. Counting coup and scalping were two battle honours. Counting coup was riding close to an enemy and touching him with a stick. Scalping was skimming off the top part of the flesh and hair on the enemy's head, usually when dead. Scalps gave the warriors status and control over the enemy's soul when dead.

Things to do

1 What did the Plains tribes want to buy from the Nez Perce?

2 a What three things changed the balance of the tribes by the early eighteenth century?

  b Why do you think they had such an impact on the native people's way of life?

By 1800, travelling to the Plains in summer to hunt buffalo had become too dangerous for the Nez Perce because they often came into conflict with other tribes. So in 1805, they decided to send an expedition hundreds of miles away to buy firearms. The expedition returned with six guns. In 1806, the American explorers Lewis and Clark sold ammunition to the Nez Perce, which might have been one practical reason for them helping the white men. Trappers and traders began to move into the territory and, by 1810, the Nez Perce had obtained enough firearms to join the Flathead in a war party of 150 that drove back the Blackfeet.

From this time, the Nez Perce were caught up in the white opening up of the west. Christian missionaries arrived and converted many Nez Perce. This meant that a division arose between those who became Christian and those who wished to live in the old traditional way – which included hunting on the Plains.

The Nez Perce painted markings on their horses which brought luck and protection in battle. The riders used Spanish saddles or rode without a saddle at all. Having a saddle and stirrups meant the rider was less likely to be knocked off his horse by a blow from a spear.

When Thomas Jefferson became President of the USA in 1801, two out of every three white Americans lived within 80 kilometres of the Atlantic Ocean. Very few white people knew anything at all about the vast expanses of America to the west. Jefferson dreamed of an expedition to reach the far Pacific Coast. The two men who led the expedition were Meriwether Lewis and William Clark. Their aim was to explore and claim land for the USA.

Lewis's and Clark's mountain crossing

By September 1805, Lewis and Clark (and the men they led) had left the Plains and were faced with crossing the mountains on their way to the Pacific. One man wrote that the mountains were as steep as the roof of a house. Horses slipped and rolled off ledges. Some just fell exhausted. Food was running short.

Through blinding snow the expedition trudged up and down the rugged mountainsides. They ate some of their horses. Later they ate a coyote, two grouse and some crayfish from a stream. One meal was just soup and tallow candles. Another was a handful of dry peas and some bear oil. By 19 September, Lewis noted in his diary that the men were showing signs of malnutrition (they had rashes and diarrhoea) and all of them were getting weaker. On 22 September, the eleventh day of the mountain crossing, they staggered out of the mountains and into the land of the Nez Perce.

Source A

This is what Joseph Whitehouse, a member of the expedition, had to say about his journey with Lewis and Clark.

16 September: When we awoke this morning to our great surprise we were covered with snow, which had fallen about two inches and it continues a very cold snow storm. Captain Clark shot at a deer but did not kill it. We mended up our moccasins. Some of the men without socks wrapped rags on their feet, and loaded up our horses and set out without anything to eat.

Source B

This is William Clark's account of 16 and 17 September.

16 September
I have been wet and as cold in every part as I ever was in my life. Indeed I was at one time fearful my feet would freeze in the thin moccasins which I wore.

17 September
The want of food together with the difficulty of passing these mountains has dampened the spirits of the party.

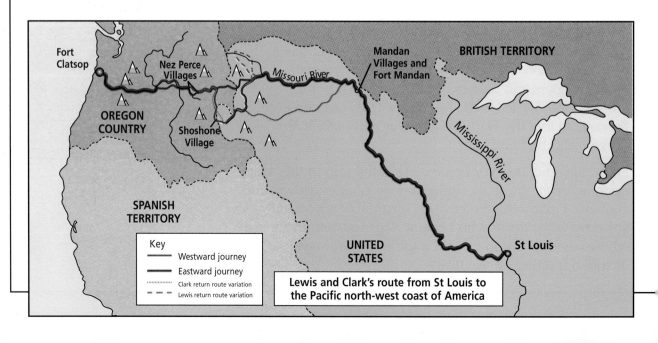

Lewis and Clark's route from St Louis to the Pacific north-west coast of America

Meeting the Nez Perce

The Nez Perce had never seen white people. Their leaders were out on a war party, so the chief who was there and his band had to decide what to do with these weak, light-coloured strangers who had suddenly arrived. According to the tribe's oral tradition, some of the Nez Perce proposed killing the white men and taking their goods. The rifles alone would have brought them great wealth. However, an old woman spoke up. She said that as a young girl, she had been captured by an enemy tribe on the Plains who then sold her to another tribe farther east and then to a white French Canadian by whom she had a child. This man had treated her kindly, and although she escaped and made her way back to her own people, she thought well of him. She opposed the killing of Lewis and Clark, saying that these were the same light-skinned people who had helped her.

The chief, Twisted Hair, then urged his people to provide the expedition with food. The half-starved men gorged themselves on salmon and camas bulbs, and were promptly ill. But when they recovered the Nez Perce showed them how to make canoes by hollowing out trees with fire. By 7 October, the expedition was ready to launch the canoes and head down river from the high Plateau to the Pacific. The Nez Perce promised to look after their horses among their own herds, until they returned in the spring and Twisted Hair accompanied Lewis and Clark for the first part of the journey.

A photograph of the Nez Perce about 80 years after Lewis and Clark met them.

Things to do

1 Where did most white Americans live in 1801?

2 Look at the text, and Sources A and B. What difficulties did the expedition encounter in crossing the mountains to find the Nez Perce?

3 If the Nez Perce had decided to kill Lewis and Clark, would this have made any difference to the eventual fate of the Native Americans?

The Nez Perce built different types of houses. On the Plateau, the houses could be either conical or long in shape. On the Plains, they often lived in tipis.

Conical houses

To build these houses, three poles were put up to form a tripod. Then a further seven or nine poles were leant around the tripod to make a strong frame. This frame was covered with woven rush mats. The end result looked like one of the tipis of the Plains tribes, although it was usually smaller.

During the winter, four or five layers of mats were added and the whole structure was sunk about half a metre into the ground. Earth was piled up around the edges so the bottom metre of the tipi was effectively underground. Skins were often hung around the inside to keep it even warmer. Although these dwellings were usually small and used by one family, they could be as large as ten metres across. Sometimes several conical houses were joined together by extending the matting roofs.

Long houses

The Nez Perce also built long wooden houses. When Lewis and Clark visited Neeshnepahkeook, a Nez Perce chief, they found the entire village of 38 families living in two large wooden houses. The houses had a wooden framework which allowed a space along the whole of the top of the roof for the smoke to escape. Wooden poles were leaned on each side with long mats attached to them like giant tiles on a roof that went right down to the ground. Dry grass protected the bottom of the mats from the earth that was stacked up to keep out draughts. More poles were leant against the mats to protect them from the wind.

The houses seen by Lewis and Clark may not have been permanent dwellings. A number of tribes built houses similar to these but usually they were temporary camps for when they gathered together to trade or to fish. The advantage of the long houses was that they needed fewer mats than a large number of tipis for individual families, so they were quicker and easier to build. Later explorers noted the same communal houses for trade gatherings and ceremonies for both religion and war.

Source A

An extract from a book about the Lewis and Clark expedition, in which the two men describe some native housing.

At a little distance from us are two houses, one of which contains eight families, and the other, which is by much the largest we have ever seen, is inhabited by at least 30. It is rather a kind of shed built, like all the other huts, of straw and mats in the form of the roof of a house, 156 feet long and about 15 wide, closed at the ends, and having a number of doors on each side. The vast interior is without partition, but the fire of each family is kindled in a row along the middle of the building.

Things to do

1 How were the Nez Perce conical houses built?

2 Why did Lewis and Clark think that the Nez Perce lived communal lives?

3 Why do you think Lewis and Clark might have been mistaken?

4 What were the advantages of Plains tipis compared with the conical houses of the Nez Perce?

Summer houses on the Plains

The Nez Perce, who went down to the Plains in summer, soon bought buffalo hide tipis from the Plains tribes. These were lighter and easier to carry on hunting and trading expeditions than the mat-covered conical houses of the Plateau. However, the Nez Perce always retained their habit of making larger houses when they were back on the Plateau and wished to have a communal place to meet.

A Plains-style tipi. Despite the hole at the top, they were smoky inside and many older people suffered from eye trouble.

4.5 HUNTING BUFFALO

The painting on these pages shows a buffalo hunt in action. Much of the summer on the Plains was spent hunting the millions of buffalo which lived there. The buffalo became even more important to the tribes all around the Plains from the mid-

Source A

eighteenth century when the use of horses became widespread. As you will see on pages 52 and 53, the buffalo was vital to the Native American way of life and could provide everything that was necessary for a nomadic existence.

Things to do

1 What weapons are being used to kill the buffalo in the picture?

2 This picture was painted in the nineteenth century. What does the artist think of the men who are hunting the buffalo?

3 How do you think men would have hunted buffalo before they had horses?

The hunt

In 1800, there may have been as many as 60 million buffalo on the Plains. At first men had hunted them on foot. One way to capture them was to drive some into an enclosure or over a cliff. However, hunting them from horseback was more reliable and provided more animals. Once a number of animals had been killed, the men leapt from their horses and began to cut up the meat. Then they loaded it on to horses and went back to camp. Sometimes the women met them on the way and once back at camp the women and the children did the unloading, often eating and roasting the best bits as they worked. The meat was cut up for eating or for drying in the sun to be used later on.

Tanned hide (soft leather) was used for tipi covers, robes, moccasins, trousers and saddle blankets.

Rawhide (hard leather) was used for belts, bags, horse harness, ropes and shields.

Dung was dried for fuel.

Tail was made into a decoration or fly swat.

Fur was made into sleeping blankets and winter clothes.

Stomach was made into cooking vessels and containers.

Fat was used as soap and for cooking.

Hooves were used for glue, tools and rattles.

Every part of the buffalo was used. The parts such as the liver, which quickly went bad, were eaten straightaway.

Flesh was eaten raw (tongue and liver) or otherwise cooked or dried for later use.

Cleaning and softening the skins

The women stretched the skins out on the ground and used flints to scrape off the meat. (After the white people came they used metal tools.) When it was dry, the skin was turned over and the hair scraped off the other side. The next job was to soften the skin which was done by rubbing boiled brains and liver on it. Then the skin was folded for a few days before being stretched on a frame, scraped, washed and rubbed with sandstone. The last job was to pull the skin over plaits of sinew to make it even softer.

Brain was used in the tanning process.

Tongue was used as a hairbrush or food.

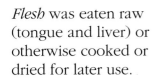

Hair was used as wool padding for saddles and pillows, rope and clothing decoration.

Bones were used to make tools, needles, arrow heads, sledge runners and dice. Bone marrow was eaten raw or cooked.

Things to do

1 What was used in the tanning process?

2 It has been said that the horse was a long-term disaster for the Native American who came to rely on the buffalo and gave up other ways of procuring food and goods.

   a Is there any essential that is not provided on the list of buffalo raw materials?

   b Why do you think it was dangerous to rely on such a large roving animal in nineteenth-century North America?

Source A

The Nez Perce lived in an area where the fishing grounds weren't very good. So they were used to supplementing their diet by some hunting and gathering of berries, bulbs and fruits. However, they lived in ideal horse country and once they acquired horses, their lives changed to being wealthy hunters who could regularly travel long distances from their homes.

The horses and the horsemen

The horses flourished on the high grasslands and protected valleys. From the moment they had horses, the Nez Perce bred selectively by castrating the poorer stallions in the herd and selling inferior animals to neighbouring tribes. In this way they built up herds numbering many hundreds of horses, that were fast, sure-footed and had plenty of stamina. The Nez Perce soon became excellent horsemen. They rode over the plateau hunting antelope, or to the mountains for deer, elk, bear and mountain sheep. Family groups rode to the camas meadows to collect the bulbs and fruit.

The Nez Perce rode with or without saddles. When riding with saddles they used a Spanish-style saddle built on a wooden frame covered with rawhide. The high back and front were covered with a soft hide and the centre, or sitting part, covered with cloth. Both saddles and bridles might be decorated with bead work.

Horse trading

The Nez Perce rode to trade meetings and added horses to the list of goods that were traded. They traded the horses they did not want. The horses they kept were the gentle type used as pack horses and for women and old people to ride. They also kept their best horses. These were reserved for men and were divided into two types. There were the comfortable, sure-footed animals for travelling over the mountains. Then there were the aristocrats of the herd, the buffalo hunters and war horses. To be included in this select group, a horse had to be able to give a buffalo a head start of about 400 metres and overtake the buffalo by about 3 kilometres. The horses were trained to approach the buffalo (which weighed all of one tonne and was fast, frightened and angry) without guidance from the rider, until they were so close the man could touch the buffalo with his foot. With the arrow discharged into the buffalo, the horse veered away to avoid the lethal horns for both horse and rider. Such horses were not for sale.

Short bows

The other thing for which the Nez Perce became famous among other buffalo hunters on the Plains was their short bows, which were easy to use from horseback and powerful enough to put an arrow through the paunch of a buffalo. Several cases were recorded in which calves running close to their mothers were killed by the same arrow that slew the mother. To buy a good bow from the Nez Perce cost the same as a good horse.

Returning to the Plateau

After a summer living in tipis on the plains, hunting buffalo, mixing and trading (or fighting) other groups, the Nez Perce mounted their second best horses, loaded their pack animals and, leading their best horses, headed back over the mountain passes before the snow came. Their pack horses carried buffalo skins and dried meat. They also carried beautiful robes made of soft tanned buffalo skin, decorated with beads and porcupine quill work. The very best were made by the Crow and could cost a good horse plus a well-made leather shirt. Once they arrived back at the settlements on the high plateau, they settled down for winter.

Things to do

1 How did the Nez Perce come to own such good horses?

2 What did the best horses have to be able to do?

3 Read Source B. What was special about the colouring of the Appaloosa horse?

4 Why could the arrival of the horse in North America be compared to the invention of the steam locomotive in Britain?

Source A

The Oregon Trail.

The Lewis and Clark expedition in 1806 brought the first white men into Nez Perce country. Other explorers, traders and fur trappers followed. Their superior tools and weapons led the Nez Perce to the conclusion that they must learn the white men's ways. In 1831, they sent a delegation to St Louis to ask for teachers. Several Christian missionaries were sent to the Nez Perce, including Henry Spalding and his wife Eliza.

Teaching the Nez Perce 'white' ways

The Spaldings taught several hundred of the tribe to read and to write. They organised a church. They also taught families how to raise sheep and pigs, and grow grain and vegetables. From the beginning, the more conservative families liked this way of life, combining it with their traditional salmon fishing and camas collecting. But the adventurous young men who preferred to race horses, gamble and go on the war path, poked fun at the stay-at-homes. They would ride by the garden patches on hot summer days and invite their farmer friends to stop what they called '**squaw** work', catch their best horses, then hunt or race with them. To the annoyance of Henry Spalding, the farming men often did. But life was changing.

The Oregon Trail

By 1850 it was a common sight to see the covered wagons wending their way westward loaded with white settlers seeking a new life in the west. The Oregon Trail started in eastern Kansas and ended on the west coast in Oregon and California. By the 1860s the journey that took six months by wagon took five to six days by railway.

Settlers on the Nez Perce lands

More white settlers were beginning to appear. In 1847, wagons carrying 4000 white people along the Oregon Trail brought not only themselves but also an epidemic of measles. Like all Native Americans, the Nez Perce and their neighbours had no **immunity** against such outside diseases. Over half the Cayuse tribe died and, fearful that their missionary was poisoning them, the Cayuse killed him and eleven others. As a result, the Spaldings fled from the Nez Perce and brought soldiers into the area. A **treaty** with the United States government, in 1855, defined the Nez Perce lands. However, this treaty became worthless in 1860, when gold was discovered on this land. Anticipating trouble, another treaty was presented to the Nez Perce, reducing their land even more. Some agreed to it. Some did not.

Meanwhile not only gold diggers but also white farmers were settling along the edges of the Nez Perce **reservation**. They turned their cattle and horses out and these roamed into the unfenced Nez Perce land. The settlers complained about the Nez Perce horses eating up the grass (on Nez Perce land) and breeding with their plodding farm horses. The new agent on the reservation was John Montieth. Like the Spaldings, he wanted to discourage the old ways of the tribe, teach them to be farmers and give up long hair, fast horses and tribal costumes. He got permission to use the army to round up all the Nez Perce and put them in just one treaty reservation. This was when he came across the Wallowa band of the Nez Perce led by their young chief, Joseph.

Source B

An extract from Captain George Currey's report 1863.

Chiefs were debating the terms of the proposed treaty in an effort to reach some compromise, but neither group would yield. Finally convinced there was no hope of agreement, they decided that the proper action was to disband the tribe, each chief becoming an independent leader of his own village. They declared the Nez Perce nation dissolved. I withdrew my detachment having witnessed the extinguishment of the last council fires of the most powerful Indian nation on the sunset side of the Rocky Mountains.

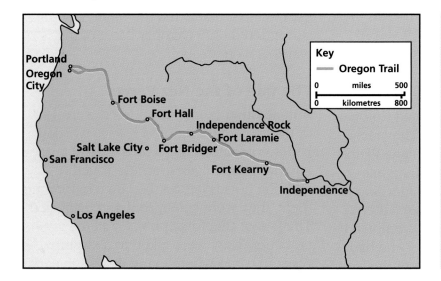

Key

— Oregon Trail

| 0 | miles | 500 |
| 0 | kilometres | 800 |

Portland
Oregon City
Fort Boise
Fort Hall
Independence Rock
Fort Laramie
Salt Lake City • Fort Bridger
San Francisco
Fort Kearny
Independence
Los Angeles

Things to do

1 Why did the Nez Perce decide to send a delegation to St Louis in 1831?

2 What did the Spaldings do?

3 Why do you think white people often disliked 'long hair, fast horses and tribal customs'?

Joseph and his band pastured several thousand horses and cattle between the Wallowa Mountains and the Snake River Canyon in north-eastern Oregon. As the army prepared to escort the band to the reservation, Joseph began a hurried round-up of all their animals and headed for the Snake River Canyon. They had to swim the river in full flood, losing about 900 animals but no people. Joseph's young warriors were angry and raided some white settlements, killing some of the people. Two companies of cavalry were sent to find Joseph's band and the war was on.

Winners and losers

Although outnumbered, the Nez Perce defeated the Cavalry on 17 June. That was followed by three and a half months of hide and seek as five armies chased Chief Joseph and his band. General Howard and his soldiers (580 of them) made a surprise attack near Clearwater, but even though he only had 100 men Joseph fought him to a draw on 11 July and retreated across about 240 kilometres of rough mountains to the Bitterroot Valley of Montana. Here they were surprised by another force on 9 August and lost 89 people – including 50 women and children – but managed to get away. Retreating to northern Wyoming they looked for shelter with their old friends the Crow tribe. However, this was refused so they turned north across Montana to join the Sioux in Canada.

Thanks to the recently installed telegraph, news of their whereabouts reached Colonel Miles who prepared his troops. They raced north, then west, across the Montana Plains to intercept the band. Once again, while preparing to break camp on the morning of 30 September 1877, the Nez Perce suffered a surprise attack. Colonel Miles attempted to wipe them out in a single charge – he had 600 men to the 120 fighting men of the Nez

Source A

Chief Joseph.

Perce. But his charge was stopped short of the camp. A six-day siege followed but when reinforcements arrived for Colonel Miles, the situation was hopeless. Winter was approaching, and the freezing weather with rain and snow caused suffering on both sides. Children cried with hunger and the old people suffered silently. Only two chiefs were left alive. Of these, White Bird escaped to Canada and the other, Joseph, surrendered on 5 October. Most of the warriors were dead.

The fate of the Nez Perce

Among other items surrendered were 1100 of their toughest, hardiest horses which had accompanied them on the 2800 kilometre nightmare journey. Together with the horses left on the range before the flight, they were taken, sold and dispersed. The fate of Chief Joseph's Nez Perce was no better. They were taken to a swampy place to camp where many died of malaria.

Source B

An adaptation of the speech that Chief Joseph made when he went to Washington in 1879 to ask the US government for better land for his people.

I have shaken hands with a great many friends, but there are some things I want to know which no one seems able to explain. I cannot understand how the government sends a man out to fight us, as it did General Miles, and then breaks his word (Colonel Miles had hoped for Joseph's band to return to the reservation). Such a government has something wrong about it. I cannot understand why so many chiefs are allowed to talk so many different ways, and promise so many different things.

I have heard talk and talk, but nothing is done. Good words do not last long until they amount to something. If the white man wants to live in peace with the Indian he can live in peace. Treat all men alike. Give them all an even chance to live and grow. I only ask of the government to be treated as all other men are treated. If I cannot go to my own home, let me have a home in some country where my people will not die so fast. Let me be a free man – free to travel, free to stop, free to work, free to trade where I choose, free to choose my own teachers, free to follow the religion of my fathers, free to think and talk and act for myself – and I will obey every law.

I have asked some of the great white chiefs where they get their authority to say to the Indian that he shall stay in one place, while he sees white men going where they please. They cannot tell me.

They were then given a reserve in Kansas where more died. They found the heat intolerable. Joseph kept petitioning and they were moved again. But they never regained land in the Wallowa Valley where he came from. Chief Joseph died in 1904.

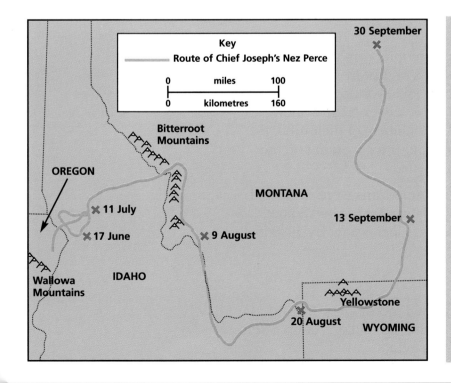

Key

Route of Chief Joseph's Nez Perce

0   miles   100

0   kilometres   160

30 September

Bitterroot Mountains

OREGON

MONTANA

11 July

13 September

17 June

9 August

Wallowa Mountains

IDAHO

Yellowstone

20 August

WYOMING

Things to do

1 Write briefly what happened on the following dates: 11 July, 9 August, 30 September and 5 October 1877.

2 What happened to Chief Joseph's band?

3 Read Source B. What freedoms does Chief Joseph want in his speech?

4 Why do you think the great white chiefs would not allow Indians to go where they pleased?

Christopher Columbus landed in the Americas in 1492. At that time there was a population of many millions scattered across the Americas. But over the next 400 years, the native population went down to less than 250,000. By the early part of the twentieth century, it seemed likely that the Native Americans would cease to exist. They became known as the 'vanishing Indians'.

Problems

Most Native Americans died from disease. When the whites came they brought diseases such as smallpox, tuberculosis, measles and even influenza which sometimes killed as many as nine out of every ten people in a tribe. Native Americans had no immunity against European diseases. White people also drove the native people from their lands. By 1900, the Native Americans were vanishing. Children were sent to schools where they learnt only English. They began to forget the old tribal life. Some tribes lived in reservations, which were large areas of land that were set aside for the tribes to live on. Often these reservations were on poor land that no white settlers wanted or they were far away from the tribes' original land and roots. Sometimes they farmed but it was very different and many found it disorientating as they were cut off from their old way of life. This could lead to problems of depression and alcoholism.

Cities

As cities began to grow, native people went there to find work. One group made a success of this. In 1886, twelve men from the Mohawk tribe got jobs working on high buildings and bridges. They were very good at working at great height. They taught other members of their tribe. By the 1930s the Mohawks were famous for working on the **skyscrapers** in New York.

For most of the time the Native Americans were neglected. But things have changed. The Native Americans did not disappear. Today the population is increasing. By 1998 it was about 2.5 million.

Living today

The Native Americans have gained more rights. In 1991, the Canadian government agreed with the Inuit to set up a **self-governing** Inuit area called Nunavut.

Some of the things that have changed.

- 1946: The US Indian Claims Commission dealt with **treaties** between the government and the native people.

- 1951: The Indian Act in Canada gave rights to native people about things like education, fishing and holding ceremonies.

- From the 1960s the US and Canadian governments gave money for tribal schools.

- In the 1970s legal help groups were set up. For instance, the Lakota (a Plains tribe) won a $105 million claim against the government for a broken treaty.

A Native American working in a gambling casino owned by his tribe.

Other tribes such as the Cherokee have set up their own organisations. The Navajo is a tribe in Arizona. They live on the largest reservation in the United States. They live in their traditional ways and earn money from making jewellery.

Rights over their own land, 1988

There are problems. It is difficult for tribes to decide how much to live in the modern American way. For instance, a law was passed in 1988 which gave native people rights over their own land. Some tribes decided to open gambling casinos. These have been very successful. The profits are used to pay for better housing, health and education. However, some people say the gambling will have a bad effect on the people of the tribe.

Things to do

1 Why was only learning English at school very serious for passing on of tribal customs?

2 What were some of the problems with reservations?

3 Look at the information box. Why do you think it took until the 1970s for the Lakota to sue the government for a broken treaty?

4 What do you think the bad effects of running gambling casinos might be?

GLOSSARY

Allegiance loyalty or friendship particularly in war

Astronomy the study of stars and other things in space

Cache store, often of food

Camas an edible bulb, eaten by the Nez Perce

Fleece coat of wool from an animal such as a sheep

Immunity resistant to disease

Irrigation works building canals to water fields

Man-of-war a warship in the days of sailing ships

Myth traditional story such as telling how the world began

Permafrost where the ground is permanently frozen

Pilgrim a person who travels usually to a holy   place (the Pilgrim Fathers were English people who travelled to America to settle there. They were religious people)

Regalia things that show a person is important or royal such as a crown

Reservation a place reserved for the native people to live in North America

Ritual a set way of doing things, particularly in ceremonies

Self-governing when a country or people rule themselves

Skyscraper very tall building

Squaw a Native American woman, particularly a wife

Status rank or position of importance

Travois a frame for carrying things that is pulled behind a horse or dog

Treaty an agreement between countries

Wolverines an Arctic animal with thick fur, hunted by the Inuit

INDEX